# Dingoes

## Victoria Blakemore

Copyright info/picture credits

Cover, Arun Sankaragal/Shutterstock; Page 3, Sciffler/Pixabay; Page 5, WITTE-ART.com/AdobeStock; Page 7, Bill Dunshea/AdobeStock; Page 9, Chris Putnam/Adobestock; Pages 10-11, NoraDoa/AdobeStock; Page 13, Susan Flashman/Shutterstock; Page 15, TahliArtPhotography/Pixabay; Page 17, Memory Catcher/Pixabay; Page 19, beau/AdobeStock; Page 21, Susan Flashman/Shutterstock; Page 23; Nicholas Toh/Shutterstock; Page 25, Christian Musat/AdobeStock; Page 27, DB543/Pixabay; Page 29, John Carnemolla/Shutterstock; Page 31, Burning_Feet_Reiseblog/Pixabay;  Page 33, Arun Sankaragal/Shutterstock

# Table of Contents

# What Are Dingoes?

Dingoes are mammals that are related to dogs. They are also thought to be related to Asian wolves.

There are three kinds of dingoes. They differ in the color of their fur and where they live.

Most dingoes are a sandy yellow color, but some can be a darker orange-red, tan, or even black.

# Size

Dingoes are about the size

of medium-sized dogs.

When fully grown, they

weigh between twenty and

forty pounds.

They are usually between

three and four feet long.

Their tail can add another

foot to their length.

Male dingoes are usually a bit

larger than female dingoes.

# Physical Characteristics

Dingoes have **flexible** wrists. They can rotate, which lets dingoes use their paws like hands. They have been seen catching prey with their paws and even opening doors.

Dingoes are able to turn their head 180 degrees. This lets them see in different directions.

Dingo fur often works as **camouflage**. It helps them blend in to the grasses and dirt of their habitat.

# Habitat

Dingoes are often found at the edge of forests, in deserts, and in grasslands.

They prefer to live close to water because it can be hard to find in parts of their habitat. Dingoes tend to stay in the same area for most of their lives.

Most dingoes live in Australia, but there are also dingoes in Southeast Asia.

In Asia, dingoes live in countries like Cambodia, China, India, and Indonesia.

# Diet

Dingoes are **carnivores**, which means they eat only meat.

Their diet is made up of kangaroos, rabbits, birds, reptiles, and rodents. They sometimes eat **livestock** such as cattle and sheep.

Dingoes have teeth that are very long and sharp. This helps them to catch and eat their prey.

Dingoes have been known to hunt alone, or in a group. They usually hunt larger animals in a group and smaller animals when they are alone.

If a dingo catches more prey than it can eat, it buries the leftovers in the dirt. Then, it comes back to eat it later.

They are most active at dawn,

dusk, and at night. The darkness

helps them to sneak up on prey.

# Communication

Dingoes use mainly sound and scent to communicate. They have a special scent they use to mark their **territory**.

They do not bark, but they do howl, snort, and growl. They do this to call other pack members or warn each other of predators that are nearby.

Dingoes also mark things with their scent by rubbing their neck or shoulders on them.

# Movement

Dingoes are intelligent and **agile**. They have been seen using their paws to open doors and climb ladders.

They are able to climb and dig quickly. They are also very good jumpers. They are hard to keep in **captivity** because they are good at escaping.

Dingoes can move at speeds of

nearly forty miles per hour. This

helps them to catch their prey.

# Dingo Pups

Dingoes have a **litter** of about five or six babies once a year. Their babies are called pups.

When they are first born, pups are kept in a space such as a hollowed out log, rocky cave, or burrow.

Pups can feed themselves after

two months. They stay with their

parents for up to a year.

# Pack Life

Dingoes are very social animals. They spend their time in groups that are called packs. A pack is often made up of about ten dingoes.

Packs travel together and hunt together. They also work together to take care of pups.

Packs are usually led by a male
and female pair. They are in
charge of the pack.

# Are Dingoes Dangerous?

In most cases, dingoes stay away from humans. However, in some places, humans feed dingoes. This can be unsafe.

There have been times when dingoes have become **aggressive** with humans. Some people have been attacked by dingoes.

Dingoes may look like dogs,

but they are wild animals. It is

better to leave them alone.

# Population

Dingoes are listed as **vulnerable**. They may soon become **endangered** if their population continues to **decline**.

Dingoes face threats such as habitat loss, hunting, and being kept as pets.

In the wild, dingoes usually live

for five or six years. They may

live as long as ten years.

# The Dingo Fence

In the 1880's, fences were used to keep dingoes away from farms. They were connected to make one large fence called the "dingo fence" in 1940.

The dingo fence runs across southeastern Australia. It is over 3,400 miles long.

The purpose of the dingo fence

is to keep dingoes away from

people's **livestock**.

# Helping Dingoes

One way people are helping

dingoes is through dingo

**sanctuaries**. They are protected

areas of land where dingoes

can live.

Some people want dingoes to

be listed as protected. They

want to prevent the hunting

of dingoes.

Preventing **conflict** between farmers and dingoes is key. The dingo fence is one way this happens. Some farmers have donkeys to help guard their **livestock**. The donkeys keep the dingoes away.

Researchers are studying dingoes. They want to know about them so they can help.

# Glossary

**Aggressive:** ready to fight, mean

**Agile:** able to move and turn quickly

**Camouflage:** using color to blend in to the surroundings

**Captivity:** animals that are kept by humans, not in the wild

**Carnivore:** an animal that eats only meat

**Conflict:** disagreement or fight

**Declining:** getting smaller

**Endangered:** at risk of becoming extinct

**Flexible:** able to bend easily

**Litter:** a group of animals born at the

same time

**Livestock:** animals such as cows or sheep

that are kept by farmers

**Sanctuaries:** pieces of land that are

protected areas for animals to live on

**Territory:** an area of land that an animal

claims as its own

**Vulnerable**: when an animal may soon

become endangered

# About the Author

Victoria Blakemore is a first grade

teacher in Southwest Florida with a

passion for reading.

You can visit her at

www.elementaryexplorers.com

# Also in This Series

| | | | | | | |
|---|---|---|---|---|---|---|
| Gray Wolves | Sloths | Flamingos | Camels | Koalas | Honey Bees | Pandas |
| Pangolins | White-Tailed Deer | Orcas | Giraffes | Corn | Meerkats | Echidnas |
| Walruses | Raccoons | Bald Eagles | Apples | Arctic Foxes | Red Pandas | Cassowaries |
| Tigers | Ladybugs | Moose | Beluga Whales | Leopards | Elephants | Jellyfish |
| Binturongs | Lions | Dolphins | Reindeer | Hammerhead Sharks | Hippos | Pumpkins |
| Peafowl | Chameleons | Florida Panthers | Aye-Ayes | Black Bears | Cheetahs | Manatees |
| Gingerbread | Polar Bears | Hot Chocolate | Orangutans | Coyotes | Marshmallows | Strawberries |

Victoria Blakemore

# Also in This Series

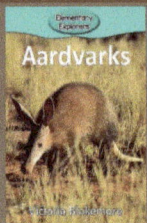

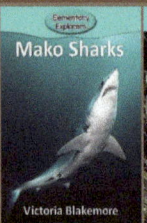

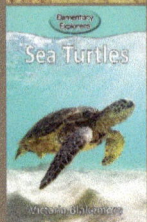

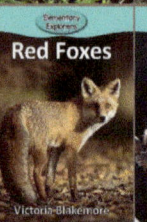

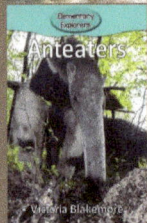

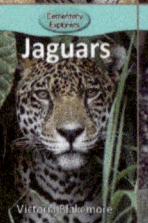

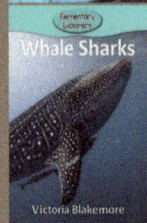

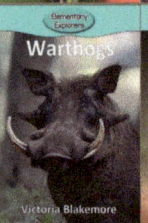

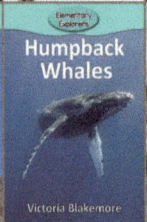

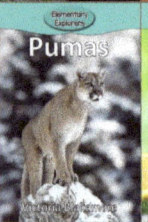

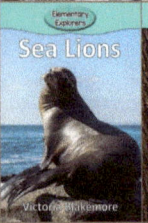

| | | | | | | |
|---|---|---|---|---|---|---|
| Aardvarks | Mako Sharks | Alligators | Frogs | Hedgehogs | Brown Bears | Bongos |
| Sea Turtles | Quokkas | Muskrats | Zebras | Red Foxes | Ring-Tailed Lemurs | Platypuses |
| Anteaters | Kangaroos | Rhinos | Jaguars | Wombats | Capybaras | Gorillas |
| Cats | Skunks | Butterflies | Dingoes | Snow Leopards | African Wild Dogs | Penguins |
| Whale Sharks | Wolverines | Warthogs | Caracals | Badgers | Seals | Hummingbirds |
| Pikas | Humpback Whales | Pumas | Lemonade | Llamas | Tulips | Ostriches |
| Sunflowers | Fennec Foxes | Sea Lions | Squirrels | Roses | Porcupines | Ice Cream |

www.ingramcontent.com/pod-product-compliance
Lightning Source LLC
Chambersburg PA
CBHW051251020426
42333CB00025B/3158